Sex
is
Not
Love

Derek Lemon

Contents

Chapter 1 The beginning

It was 1982, and as a three-year-old, I had no idea that my life would be turned upside down, I was about to be thrust into a world of sexual perversion without my permission. I believe that the devil can sense who we will become, and for some of us, he immediately attacks, but it is allowed by GOD! I was molested by three grown adults, one woman and two men, all still living, and I later found that I wasn't the only child that was violated this way.

I was a shy child already, and this did not help for years. I held my head down as I spoke, causing me to not be heard, but to be honest, most of my life, I have felt like this invisible I know now that is the lie the devil used to keep me in self-pity. I am grateful today for freedom from that untruth. I also had self-esteem issues. I thought, who could love me at all? My mother was 16 when she birthed me a child herself. My father was a married man who never was in my life.

My grandmother Jennie (R.I.P.) and grandfather L.J., as well as uncles and aunts, raised me for the first three years of my life.

The enemy had a well-laid-out plan of rejection, abandonment, and fear for my life. I understand now, at 44, what I could not comprehend all these years my parents were dealing with some stuff themselves, and I did think, why did I come this way? GOD had a wonderful plan, and despite it all, my life has not been too bad. My grandfather told me as a toddler, I would play with my male cousins for a bit and then go off on my own. My grandmother thought this was wrong and tried to change my nature, and my grandfather said no, leave him alone; he will not be like everyone else, and this is very true.

I want to share some details and experiences that lead me down the rabbit hole of trying to find love, acceptance, and peace none of these things are found outside of a real genuine relationship with GOD, our creator. I have learned God is a jealous GOD, AND he will have no other god before him. I pray that by reading my lifeline, you will see yourself in it and find solace and restoration in all of your life.

I will say it has not been easy at all because the devil is never going to leave me alone permanently, but I do have refuge in GOD through Jesus Christ, our Lord and Savior! I welcome you all to experience Sex is not love.

The Beginning

God Bless,

"D"

A child's innocence is such a pure thing, the joy, peace, and freedom it brings.

This is the blessing that Adam and Eve had until sin came in and disrupted their path.

I can relate to their former situation before perversion made an impartation, leaving me confused, abused, and used.

I am an adult now and finally facing the pain.

I pray my trials and lessons are for your gain.

Love,

"D"

Chapter 2 Fatherless (being without a father)

Let me start off by saying I did have a man physically present in my life, but that was it. He was not available spiritually or emotionally; I understand now that my dad could not give me what he did not possess himself. His father was not an emotional man at all, a man's man if you will. I had a conversation with dad about this, and he said he felt he expressed love by providing, and by man's standard, yes, that is great, but becoming a father it is a little more detailed. I must mention I hold no ill will towards my dad because of what he could not give me at that time.

I know now a child, male/female, will need to hear I love you, I am proud of you, and job well done. If the relationship is more discipline and little reward or praise, a child can grow to be hard and detached like I did not care for anyone but myself. I hid some emotions and others I could not contain and was labeled crazy for it as well. I am aware now of the huge void it left in me and it caused me to go out and try and fill it. My Dad did tell me later on he was proud of me.

I did that by becoming sexually active at 13. I should have never opened this pandora box because what I did not know then was that it would cost me dearly, and I would pay in full. I caution everyone, please don't become promiscuous like I did. It is a self-inflicted wound that takes years to heal and leaves the residue of pain for a while.

I was sexually violated three times by a brother/sister duo, not at the same time, and their first cousin was so conflicted as a child. Yes, I was under the age of 5. I had all these unnatural thoughts. I knew they were wrong, but something inside me was strong, and I eventually gave in to the temptation and fell into sexual sin. I bet some of you would be shocked to know the names of these predators, especially the women; I could bet money that they were victims of abuse as well. That is the ugly cycle. This impartation of sexual perversion caused issues in my family unit; my dad and mom had a talk with me when I was caught doing stuff with my cousins. I stopped for a while until I was old enough to go out and experiment with an older guy from school. I never wanted to have same-sex attraction internally! I knew it was wrong, and when I did act out, I was flooded with shame and guilt. I would cry out to

God and ask, why am I like this? People don't like me already,

and now this?

I want to mention that I don't blame anyone for my actions at all; I am simply telling my story to help someone else.

Fatherless

I believe that most kids, especially sons,
look to their earthly father for validation and
foundation.
I did not have this luxury;
the little boy inside of me had been tainted,
and so trust for men had been damaged
tremendously.
How can I trust a man when I never felt
protected or even
selected?
I acted out of my soulish pain and had a bad
attitude that created some internal and external
wounds.
The words I spoke were most times harsh, but
they did reflect my heart.
I am now on the road to recovery and discovery.
My identity is in the one who created me, not
any man attached to me.

Chapter 3 Hiding out

I grew up very fast. I started working at the age of 13, like a lot of Southern kids did. I worked at a place called the Pancake House in Kenly, NC, I was a dishwasher. It felt good to be able to earn my own money and to finally be able to buy name-brand shoes and not get picked on for that at school anymore. I remember one time this guy embarrassed me in a group of guys because I was wearing Converse, they were not cool to wear then. I eventually got into a fight with him and beat him up in the bathroom. We only had one eyewitness. I got tired of his big mouth, and when he challenged me, I accepted and won.

I remember this Christmas year well. It was the first sexual encounter I had with a girl I did not know what I was doing at all. I will say this young girl had way more experience. She would later get pregnant by me and did not even tell me. I only found out many years later from my cousin Hope Winston (RI.P.) I knew I had a struggle with same-sex attraction after being violated earlier in life, and it did come out in my personality and behavior as well. I was so ashamed of myself, even my own speaking voice. I wanted to change but did not know how.

I dated other girls and, at the time, did not realize it was a cover so I would not be found out, but I will say I never used anyone at all or cheated. If I was with someone, I was devoted and faithful. I met another young lady who happened to be friends with my sister. I remember coming home from Job Corp, and this girl was so pretty, but she was five years younger. I was hesitant to talk to her because she was a beautiful girl, and I was sexually active and did not want to ruin her life. I was not a fan of protection at that time.

I did relent and started dating her; when I tell you it was one of the best relationships I have had and one of the worst, let me explain. We dated as civilians only to reconnect as military members. It was funny, actually; I was on her base for school training, and I was in the line at the chow hall about to get dinner, and she said she walked in and saw my last name on my uniform pants. She said she thought of me immediately. Well, little did I know she was behind me, and I turned around and there she was still beautiful with those brown eyes.

I did not know how to feel but I knew our paths crossed for a reason once again. I will wrap this up: we started dating again, and when I got to Virginia, she was stationed in Maryland. We linked up physically for the first time, and she got pregnant. I was told later that she decided to end the pregnancy, and let me say I am not shaming her at all. I wish I had a say, but I didn't. Also, I would never reveal who she is ever so when I get to heaven, I have two kids waiting for me to meet.

I will say I was harassed a lot because of the spirit of homosexuality that was on me, and some people made me feel like a leper as well. This did nothing for my self-esteem. It hurt, it badly. I hope anyone going through this gets the support and love they need to be able to walk into their divine freedom.

Chapter 4 Family life

I have been told that a mother knows when she has a child who has homosexual tendencies. I want to tell you it is true, and I did not tell my mom face to face. She was a strict person, and I never heard her bash a gay person. I just was ashamed so I wrote a letter to her and to my surprise, she did not respond negatively at all. My struggle became clear when I invited a guy I met in Job Corps, and my feelings turned into- something else. This did not end well, and this caused an even larger hole in our family dynamic. I feel responsible that I brought this guy around; he caused some pain not just for me but for my entire family.

I take responsibility for my part in the situation, and our family has never been the same at all, even today. I was somewhat replaced by this guy, and I reverted back to the little boy who was rejected and abandoned. Sol gave away all of my household stuff and called my Aunt Blanche White (R.L.P.) in Richmond, VA, and moved there for about two years. I forgot to mention my Bio Dad did not raise me at all. In fact, I know where he lives and have his number, but we don't have a relationship at all. My mother found out he was married, and she was only 16 when she had me, she quickly ended the relationship and cut him off, and if he could not have her, he did not want me either. My father was bold because my mother and his wife attended the same school, he was a trip, right? He made a choice not to be in my life, and as a result, the damage was done internally. I am still recovering at 44. I want to say I did forgive him and have never disrespected him at all as a parent, even though absent.

Fathers and Mothers, please understand that whatever your child lacks at home, they can and will find somewhere else, and most times, it will be a detriment to themselves. I am a living witness. I want to say! I am grateful for exposure because anything we don't confront; we can't get healed and delivered from. God had a plan all along, and I did not even know it. Romans 8:28 was about to become active in my life for real!

I have had to allow God to show me myself and accept, adopt, and adjust in all areas. I asked God to show me my ugly self. Y'all, I had some deep-rooted anger issues that came out at the wrong times. I had a bad attitude, and I did not trust anyone, especially men. I would not stay at a job long if you pissed me off. I would quit and go on to the next. I was a good worker, just had a bad attitude for sure.

I got tired of being mad all the time. I can remember praying this simple prayer, and oh boy, did my life change. I prayed to God I will go where you want me to go, and I will do what you want me to do well, he heard me, and it was game on.

Chapter 5 Academics and moving on

I must say I was not a scholar in school, also I was no dummy either at all. I did graduate and did not like school, mostly because of the bullying I received. I had to go to summer school very early on, and I did not try, and while my parents (mom) Dad was on the road as a truck driver. I will say you must have patience for a child who may learn differently if not, you can shatter their self-esteem. That happened to me. I could not take getting upset because I didn't understand. I will say that any of our hurts and pains we pass along to our kids if we don't recognize and get free, and I received some pain that would take years to recover from.

I always knew that I could do more. I am a hands-on, quick learner, and I showed that in the jobs I worked. I started out in fast food chains and did get promoted at 17 at McDonald's. It was fast-paced, and I ran the back. It was fun, though I loved the challenge. I was quickly approaching graduation and did not have a clue about my future.

I did what most did and got a job and just kept going, and while it paid bills, I still felt a longing for more. I must mention I have always been different from my siblings and other family members, and I could not hide it. I was not interested in street life at all; uniquely designed. I am glad I never got caught up in following the crowd at all. So glad many have lost their lives trying to fit in.

I finally came to a point and decided to go get a trade, so I explored the option of Job Corp my mother had attended in Kentucky back after she gave birth to me. I thought I wanted to do agriculture, but once the instructor said you can't kill snakes.

I asked, "Where do I go to sign up or something different, and that was a drum roll, Culinary Arts?"

I was entering into something I was not familiar with. My mom did all the cooking, and I ate, and that was it. Oh yeah, I washed dishes as well. I was not the best cook, but I did enjoy it, and I met some really good folks. We were thick as thieves, always cutting up; people would hate to see us behind the lunch line serving. I stayed in the program for about one year and a half or so. I believe this sparked my belief that I could do better and be better.

I left there and returned home; there wasn't enough room for my parents, so I had to get my place. I stayed in NC for about a year or more, and then I moved to Richmond, VA. I lived with my Aunt Blanche White and Uncle Clarence; they are both gone now R.I.P. I was glad to be able to get a fresh start in a new city and was grateful to be out of NC for good.

I stayed here for about two years and started to get restless as if I knew my time was up there, and it was. I prayed one day, "Lord, whatever you want me to do, I will do it, and oh boy, was I in for a surprise in the form of the United States Navy."

I will mention my Aunt Hattie Stancil prophesied that I would join years before I was like, I will not join anyone's military. God made me a liar.

Chapter 6 Mirror Mirror

How many times have you met someone and immediately you all did not click? Most times, you and that person share some stronghold in common and see it in each other and don't like it. I have a younger brother, Eugene, and he and I are so much alike. I mean, he was almost born on my birthday. We are 14 years apart; when he came into the family, it was as if he was the firstborn Son. He had the affection and attention I always wanted, and of course, it made me jealous of him. He even felt my dislike for him, and I can admit now my frustrations were misdirected for sure.

He could not help that he was loved and adored, and I wasn't as loved and adored, and I was not that easy to get along with either, to be honest. I tried sabotaging my parents' marriage once, and it failed. I was a complete mess, y'all my Pastor just recently started a series on Soulish's pain and trauma and why we do what we do. I understand now how deep it is and was, and I am so thankful for this teaching.

I realize now how my parent's pain got passed down to me through generational curses, and once something goes in, it will always come out, and when it does, it is not pretty. I apologize to my little brother, and I must say he has turned out to be a great young man. I needed to face some hard truths, and God knows it would hurt like heck, and it did. I can say it made me who I am today. I needed a new attitude and mindset, which the Navy gave me, I am thankful for that time.

I must admit that during my enlisted time, I was treated better by people who did not look like me, except for this Filipino Senior Chief, who was a secret racist. I was acting out after getting diagnosed with a life-changing disease, and my cry for help was met with, I am going to write you up. I hated that duty station. I will not name it because then the guy could be identified. I am over it, but it was a very painful and empty time in my life.

I thank God for carrying me through. I had two roommates that did not work out; I believe one of them tried to get their friend to hurt me in my own home. Thank God for His protection. I have been through it with people I should have known; greater was my purpose.

As I look at you, I look at myself. I understand better than you know that you are crying out for help. Like a little child who can't speak, your words escape you, you need peace. You fight and argue to prove how strong you are, but inwardly, you know you are dead wrong. What's the use of pointing fingers? Hate just makes you meaner, and who wants to put up with that behavior? Do you realize you are sick and need help?

Help from your situation that causes frustration. I mean, it is a clear indication that peace of heart, mind, and spirit have long since taken a permanent vacation. So, you find fault in others when the plank is clearly in your eye to ignore this is simply a lie.

Mirror Mirror

Most times, what we see ugly in
others is also inside us.
We take extreme measures and
cover it with pride, and this is how
the sickness keeps spreading along.
I beg you to face the person you see
every day and ask God for help to
change the image you see.
We were never made in the image
of me.
ONLY God's image will change
and bring you victory.

Chapter 7 Brokenhearted

I can remember one Saturday morning; I was excited like it was Christmas. I had seen my birth Dad, and he promised he would come and take me shopping for gifts, and, man, I was overjoyed. Now, I will say he had made promises and not kept them, but this time was different. I waited and waited, and he did not come at all. I was devastated this time. I remember my mom telling me that I would find out who my dad was, and I learned at 11 years old, I would never have a relationship with my dad.

I now knew where he lived, and what he drove, and he even had a mother-in-law who lived down the street from me. He would visit her often. I imagine seeing him and him acting as if I did not exist. I now know my distrust of men grew that day, and I would rebel against male authority figures in my life from that moment on. The men in my life failed me at some point and I realize you can't give what you don't have ever! My relationship with men was dysfunctional, and I yearned for validation from the male species. Anytime something is out of order, it becomes twisted.

I was molested, and that turned into homosexual feelings and experiences that I was ashamed of, but I realize now that Jesus bore all of this on the cross on Calvary. I don't have to be fearful of what people say, and let me tell you a secret. If a guy or girl is always bashing a gay person, they secretly want them. I could tell you some stories from my youth. I was sexually harassed all the time by so-called heterosexual men.

Parents listen, especially men. Let your boys know that you love them, hug them, and show them affection so they will not go and try to find it in the streets because Satan always has a backup plan, like he did for himself, and we all know how that worked out. I will let my children know that they are loved and adored and made in God's image. This is vitally necessary, but again, if this has not been instilled in the adult raising you, chances are they will and can't do this.

A son needs a spiritually grounded man, not saying girls don't. I am speaking from the male perspective; a son needs a man who is not afraid to show his vulnerability and insecurities as well. I know many men were taught that men don't cry. Well, can I ask a question? Don't men feel? Do they not have any emotions floating inside them? The answer is they do. God gave us all emotions, but they are supposed to be submitted and governed by the Holy Spirit. I want to say again that I place no blame on the men in my life because I did learn from them the good, bad, and the in-between.

I am most grateful for Larry McFadden, who raised me as his own and is responsible for the great man I turned out to be, not perfect, but awesome! I appreciate him, and I try and show him whenever I can thank him. I want to tell you of the time when I was in California, and I needed a car. I called my dad and asked him to co-sign for a vehicle. He did not hesitate and said, "Well, you need a car to get around." And I got one that same day.

Chapter 8 Discovering God's hand

I love that song 'Amazing Grace' it has a line in it that says, "I once was blind, and now I see now I can truly appreciate it." The whole song, really, but that line, in particular, caught my heart. I was so blinded by what I thought was right for me. I was so very unsettled and unstable. I was a textbook definition of a vagabond, and if you don't know what that is, it means a person who wanders from place to place without a home or job. I must say the job thing is totally wrong. I have always worked, but the part that resonates with me is the wandering part.

I bought things to fill the void. I looked good on the outside, and on the inside, I was a dead man walking like so many others who don't know or recognize God's hand upon their lives at all. I was oblivious to the call, but I did see early into the spiritual world. I remember one time in our trailer for about three days, an evil spirit was just slowly walking around our home.

I was scared to death because I am a light sleeper, so every night, I heard it, and it was like it was right in the house. Back then, the trailers were paper thin. I should have known then that I had value to the Kingdom of God because of the early attacks on my life. I almost died twice in a car wreck before I was 25. I am grateful for the prayers of the saints in my life.

I eventually began to see God's hand on me and surrendered to His will, and then life got easier because of my obedience to him. I look at my life, and I am amazed at all I have accomplished. I never would have imagined how good God wanted to be to me, glad the light bulb finally came on.

Chapter 9 A change of scenery

The first time I moved away from home was for Job Corp. I was in the mountains, a place called Pisgah Forest. I enjoyed the view. I can see why I love the mountains. It was the start of a new beginning for me. I loved how peaceful and beautiful it was then. I still have a bond with three people I met there back in 1997. I started out doing horticulture, but when they said, "We could not kill snakes," I was out. I signed up to do culinary arts. Now, before you go thinking I am some master chef, I am not.

I can cook a little, man. Did we have fun in class and outside of class? I will say my friends were definitely more popular than myself. I am learning now how people whispered about me being gay, although I kept it to myself, but you want to hear facts. Some of the guys that nobody suspected where homosexual were gay in their real lives. I know three guys that were cool with everybody that were bisexual or at least curious, and no, I never hooked up with anyone, and that can be validated.

I stayed for almost two years and left and came back home. I had to get my own place because there was no room at the house for me, so I got a spot and started working at a convenience store as a cashier/cook. I thank God for Alice Hinton-Richardson (R.I.P.). She helped me get hired. I liked the job. I was the only guy there; we stayed pretty busy, too.

Well, y'all, here comes some drama. I allowed one of my Job Corp friends to come and live with me, and it was like I was replaced as a son; this person had and still has a dysfunctional relationship with their family, so my mother was truly a mother to them. I was devastated because I grew up feeling that I should have never been, and in the end, my heart was crushed after a sibling of mine started a relationship with them.

I realize now that experience pushed me into my destiny after some drama, nothing physical. I got rid of everything in my home in Kenly, NC, and I moved to Richmond, VA, for about two years. I believe God used this situation to get me out of my comfort zone, and it worked.

I will say this is the first time I have been depressed and didn't care about anything. I am glad I was not suicidal at all, thank God. I was a wreck mentally and emotionally, though. I was working a great job at Bayer Aspirin and could have gotten hired, but I stayed out a week as a temporary worker and eventually quit.

I did not know it then, but my life was about to do a 180 degree in more ways than one.

Chapter 10 What are you doing? Where are you going?

After being in Richmond, VA, for a while, I felt like I was moving on with my life while this was true physically. I know now that this was not true emotionally, spiritually, and mentally. I can think back on the situation that caused me to move, and each time, it brought up uncomfortable feelings. I had not faced the truth about myself and the situation. I was in for a rude awakening, and I know now the ugly truth is better than a beautiful lie.

My issues were deep-rooted internally, and no outside thing can be a root of anger, rage, hate, loneliness, fear, etc. My geographic location did not automatically cure me at all. I remember I had to come back to N.C. to pay license fees so I could get a VA license, and guess who did I run into? My mom and the friend I had the falling out with. I can say this was an uncomfortable situation, to say the least. I felt the same anger I felt when I left N.C.

I can thank God now because he used that situation to push me into my destiny! I just didn't know it at the time. I can remember praying to God a simple prayer, and that catapulted me into His perfect will. I repented for the sins I committed against God with a sincere heart. I honestly felt like I was sinking in the sand, being out of God's will. I felt a shift almost instantly after that prayer. It got uncomfortable for me at 1510 Presson Blvd, and it was time to go.

I moved back to N.C. for about three months, joined the Navy, and was off into God's perfect will. My family dynamic still was a hot mess. I still was an outcast, and I did have a bad attitude and was angry, so I understand now why no one wanted a relationship with me. I longed for a connection and looked for it in all the wrong places. I felt like I was just going to have to push through by myself! I was deceived, really.

I hated my first duty station. The only good thing was I made a couple of time friends, and that made it bearable. I was ecstatic to leave from there. I did get my only Navy Achievement Medal there. I can recall my supervisors set me up to fail, and it backfired on them. Romans 8:28. I must behonest that the people who looked like me were mostly against me, not all, but most.

I can admit my attitude was not the greatest, but I have always been a good worker and followed the rules to the letter. I was strong-willed and did not like being taken advantage of at all. I hate injustice and will speak up when needed. I got settled in, and a year passed, and my mother had a massive stroke and has not recovered at all after all those years. My mother did something strange; she would cry when I would leave her. She did not do this with anyone else. Our relationship had not been mended, but my mom did apologize to me, and I think I did, too.

My father and I have subsequently reconciled, who did not understand me at all, but somewhat he does now. I see how God had to separate me to make me see and not point the finger at anyone else. Satan will always have you focus on others but God is trying to get you to see you.

Befler Days

Like the wind changes direction, my Father, God
has a plan and it is perfection.
Like many famous artists known to man,
with the stroke of their brush, a masterpiece is at
hand.
GOD is the same way; he is the master potter.
We are the clay.
GOD never promised any rainy days, but he did
give the rainbow as a promise and a sign of hope
that he is always near and knows what is best.
In life, sometimes it gets dark, and the tunnel of
transformation seems long.
Just remember, the author of your story will
always get the glory,
so when it feels like too much,
give it to the one who can handle it all
and will catch you when you fall.
I guarantee there is always sunshine after the
rain and gain through pain;
Beter days are ahead.

Chapter 11 A fresh start

I was so grateful for my Aunt Blanche and Uncle Clarence for allowing me to live with them. I was so broken and just angry when I showed up at her doorstep. They took me in without hesitation, and I was grateful. The warm welcome was much needed. I felt like I had finally found a home. I immediately started looking for work and found it. I really liked living in Richmond, VA. It was something new. Let me tell you, the guys around the year 1999 were pretty bold.

I was out one night, and this dude rolled up on me while I was out with another guy. I had never had that happen, and it did happen again. While I was with my aunt, a guy tried to approach me, and I was like, nope. I will admit I was down low. I did not want anyone to know what I was doing. I was ashamed, and I could never utter the words. I am gay; it just could not come out at all.

I settled pretty well and got involved with a guy who sold drugs, and eventually, he did time. I was on the local chat line, meeting and hooking up with strangers. It was a very risky behavior and not smart because I was in places I was not familiar with, but sin will have you blind seriously. I was trying to fill a void that only God could. I met a guy who was heavily connected to the gospel music industry, and let me say I was shocked at what I was told, no judgment at all. The city was full of violence when I lived there, but I am the type of person who likes to explore, so I found my way around.

My uncle Clarence would drive me and scare me to death. One day, he almost ran into the back of someone, and when I called him out, he got mad and said, "Next time, let your aunt take you around."

I was like, "Gladly." Uncle Clarence made the best sweet potato pies and other stuff. I can't explain how good it felt to be away from NC.

I was about to have another life change and did not even know, thankfully! Obeyed.

Chapter 12 Facing harsh realities

I studied Matthew 7:1-6 this morning. Why is this important? I am glad you asked. From so long, when I looked at others, I did not see my own reflection at all. I will break it down for you. The man who raised me was a good man but super passive with my mother. He did not lead as a man should have. My father did provide but he would not make the decisions a man should have to properly lead his family. I am by no means judging or disrespecting my father at all. I am simply stating my experience growing up, how it affected me as a young man, and how it shaped my relationship with women early on.

My father came from a two-parent home, and his dad was a manly man and did not show emotions. Kids generally follow the example set before, whether it is good or bad. I took some good and bad from him as well. I am grateful for all he taught me because, for the most part, I turned out alright. I know now children learn what they live and what has lived before them always. I pray one day to be a better example because I know what effect being a bad one has left on me.

I will now tell you about my mother. She was a teen when she got pregnant at 15 by a young man a little older than her. I could only imagine being so young and being involved with an older guy now. I do believe the relationship was consensual. My father was a married man and this has caused drama. I don't place blame on anyone, but I will say this was a whole mess. I used to think, why did I come here this way?

But believe me, God knew how and when I would get here. I used to be ashamed of the fact, but not anymore because I know now I have a purpose for being here, and it is coming to fruition.

I beg parents, please get healed and delivered of childhood trauma before having kids. Getting therapy is not a bad thing at all. I believed what I was taught was taboo. To get help in my community meant you are crazy. Not all feel that way, but a good portion of folks do. I want to share a plaque that hung in our old home as a family. It is so befitting to raise children. I hope it sheds light on the toxic traits and positive traits we pass along to our seeds.

"Children learn what they live," by Dorothy Law Nolte, Ph.D.

If children live with criticism, they learn to condemn. If children live with hostility, they learn to fight.

If children live with fear, they learn to be apprehensive.

If children live with pity, they learn to feel sorry for themselves.

If children live with ridicule, they learn to be shy. If children live with jealousy, they learn to envy.

If children live with shame, they learn to feel guilty. If children live with tolerance, they learn patience. If children live with praise, they learn appreciation. If children live with acceptance, they learn to love.

If children live with approval, they learn to lie themselves. If children live with recognition, they learn to have a goal. If children live with honesty, they learn truthfulness.

If children live with sharing, they learn generosity. If children live with fairness, they learn justice.

If children live with kindness and consideration, they learn respect.

If children live with security, they learn to have faith in themselves and in those around them.

If children live with friendliness, they learn the world is a nice place in which to live.

I agree with all except the last two. Our faith is to be in God and Him alone. Also, the world is not a nice place to live in, especially now, but I respect her perspective. I look back at my childhood, and my parents gave me some of both the good and the bad, and now, at 45, I am sitting out the negative. This just does not begin either. I remember when I was younger, I was labeled crazy, and I still am to some. I did not communicate with my family. I felt like an outsider who had been placed in the wrong family. I know now God is very Intentional, and he knew what I needed to gain from my family unit. I am grateful and love my family and can accept now our paths are just different.

After I took a close internal look at myself and got honest, I realized that I hated who I was. I despised having a bad attitude and a negative outlook on life. I felt like a pressure cooker that could explode at any given minute. I was truly messed up in my emotions and displayed it in my daily life

and activities. I did not know where to start to heal. Who could trust? Who could I be vulnerable to without being

judged and ostracized? I desperately needed and wanted to release all this pain, rejection, abandonment, and fear so I could be whole.

I suffered on the inside, but I know now that what is going on inside always shows up outside. It's like a self- reflecting mirror. I was a bit anti-social because of my low self- esteem as well. Some may think well, he never showed it; people tend to guard against pain. I was good at camouflage and could blend in very well. I remember when my mother would send me to the store and I would take the long way to avoid the neighborhood boys if they were out to not get picked on.

I was a skinny guy with a big butt. I hated it a lot because some of the guys would actually grab my butt, and they were supposedly heterosexual. I later found out that one of the most popular guys in the neighborhood wanted to sleep with me. The words used were that he was infatuated with me. I did not know the meaning of it at the time, but it sounded creepy this same guy would pull out his manhood and flash

me and my sister. I was sexually harassed and did not even know it. I did have same-sex attraction, but I was also scared to act on it, but I eventually did with an older guy at my school. He picked me up one day, and we fornicated in his car.

I can't say it was a good experience. It was just an

experience, and I did not see him again. He soon left our school. I would not ever have close male friends because my feelings would turn erotic, and to be honest, they did not have that on their agenda at all. I have since been able to be friends with a man and not go there at all. I was allowing my flesh to take over, and soon, the appetite to explore affections between myself and another male overtook me, and I caved.

I must say that even in the act, I was ashamed of what I was doing. I knew it went against what God's law is, and yet it was like a spiritual stronghold that captivated me, and I could not resist temptation at all. My reckless one-night stands caught up to me in 2006. It was kind of ironic I had prayed to God at a gay club in D.C. I asked God to take away the desire, and that I did not want to do this anymore, and when January 2006 rolled around, my life changed drastically.

I was diagnosed with a life-changing disease, and I was shocked to my core. I had never had any type of disease at all. I was told by the doctor when he told me that I act like I am surprised. I honestly wanted to punch his lights out bad. I would have ended up in the Brigg Sol refrained from doing so. I was in denial for about six months, and then it hit me like a ton of bricks all at once: I began to be depressed about my life and future. God had made a promise to me that I would get married and have a family. How is this going to happen now?

I was mad at God, but I should have been mad at myself for being so careless. Sin is fun for a season, but the price is always higher than what you are willing to pay. I know now that I did not receive a death sentence spoiler alert. I did get married to a natural-born woman. This life change set me on the road to God processing me so I could become the minister that I am today.

Chapter 13 Loneliness

I remember using this saying a lot that I could be in a room full of people and still feel alone. I wonder how many people have felt like this. I always felt invisible. This feeling started as a little boy. I was a shy child and was not like my male cousins. I had gifts and talents they did not possess, so I thought surely God made a few mistakes on me, and I desperately wanted to be like them; I just could not. I felt like I did not have a voice for an exceptionally long time. I would speak with a mumble and did not look people in the face when I spoke to them.

My self-esteem was low, and it was for quite a while. This broken little boy was still being pieced together again. I would not wish anything I experienced on anyone else but myself. I realized I was empowered to live and grow through it. I was a loner as a child as well. Let me tell you what my grandfather, whom I called Daddy, said about me as a toddler. He said, "I would often be playing with my two male cousins, and after a while, I would go by myself." My grandmother, whom I called Moma, thought this was strange, and my Daddy told her that it was my nature to go my own way, and sure enough, that has been my life.

I am the third oldest grandchild, the only one of the five raised with my grandparents who went into military service, like my aunt and uncles. I might add that I was the least likely to join the military; the idea of someone yelling at me and in my face was a no for me and the money whew, if you know you know. I did not have money, and the struggle was real. My life did get better, and God did work some things out of me. I did learn to listen to authority. I can imagine God saying if you will not listen to man, you will not listen to me at all.

I did survive eight years of not getting into trouble in the Navy. Thank God I did have some close calls, but all went well. I wanted to touch on how males always treated me wrong and vastly different, and I felt it, too. It was like I disgusted them. I did have feminine ways, and that was it. I hated that as well. My voice was high-pitched, and I sounded like a girl! I did not have my dad around until my teens because he worked as a truck driver long distance and was only home on the weekends.

God had to shatter my belief about what a father is. My experiences had not been the greatest, and I did push back on genuinely connecting with the man who raised me because the one who made me rejected me. Many people are broken boys and girls because they did not get the love they needed as a child. It does make a difference. I will let my children know they are loved and that I am a safe place for them to come to. The result of a loveless child will produce a void in the child's heart, and they will fill it with everything they can think of and mostly to their detriment.

Chapter 14 Wait a minute, not so fast

This is a public service announcement. If you have lived a certain way your whole life and then come to Christ, your life will not just change overnight. I am not saying God can't deliver instantly because he can. I am warning of a zeal spirit. You feel like you are on top of the world and can take o anyone or anything we must do as the word instructs and fill ourselves with the word, prayer, fasting, and meditation on the word as well. The enemy of our soul will send spirits back to see if the house they came from is full or empty. If it is empty, they will come back with seven demons stronger than themselves, and that person will be worse off than before.

I put myself in a situation that caused me to be vulnerable.

I was deceived, and I helped get there. I thank God for showing me I was not as strong as I thought I was and that I still had some reside there. Satan just needs a small opening to come in. The Bible tells us he goes to and from seeking whom he may devour. His attacks are very intentional. We must suit up daily with the word of God so that we will be always able to stand against the wiles of the devil and his schemes, John 10 tells us the devil comes to steal, kill, and destroy if we do not have value then he would not waste his time the enemy knows he has very little time left.

I want to encourage everyone reading this that you may fall, but get back up and, in the game, don't ever quit, no matter what it looks like. I have had to encourage myself on many occasions not to lose heart. The weight of life can bog you down, but God told us to cast our care upon him, for he cares for us notice how it says care singular. Life will happen, and we can't get by the persecutions, the tests, and the trials that come to make us strong. I welcome God's grace to help me face whatever I must face.

I remember that my low self-esteem led me to some desperate places and faces, allowing me to connect with

people I should have never met. I realize now the root of the issue, folks. There is always a root to everything alcoholism, for my grandfather might have been because he married young and did not have a father figure to direct him. I can fill in the blanks about what caused the habit or sin to form. I am grateful for being able to be honest; that is what brings freedom.

I could never really get free until I got honest with myself and then with God. He loves to confess he already knows and is standing, waiting to rescue us each time.

Chapter 15 Dreaming

For years now, I have had these visions and dreams about my wife. I could never see her face. I remember her hair and skin tone, but that is it. I have seen little girls. I have always said no to little girls because I am overprotective for real, but whatever healthy and happy child he sends, I will be okay with it. I sit sometimes and visualize our little family hanging out at home doing nothing, just spending quality time with each other. I believe this very simple act has been outdated, the misuse of technology has hurt us all. I want and need my home to be filled with love, laughter, silliness, and comfort. I want anyone who visits to feel the welcoming spirit we have. I used the poem Children live what they learn, and they are indeed little sponges.

I can recall being around a lot of adults who cursed like sailors, and guess what? I grew up swearing like one as well and was good at it. Back to dreaming. I also want to write songs and maybe some short films or something creative. I want to live outside of the US for most of the year and have my kids experience stuff I never did as a child, as well. I want them to leave home and know that they are loved and that they can return if need be. I also have a passion for male veterans, the ones of color, because they sometimes have a difficult time getting what they need from the very system they honorably served. Speaking from experience, our white counterparts usually get disability help before they exit active duty.

I am not biased and will help everyone. I am just saying that the veterans need safe places to live and jobs where they can make a livable wage and take care of themselves. Most don't want handouts at all. I used the system myself and am grateful for the help I received when I needed it. I know God will allow me to help others because that is my heart's desire. I also want to buy my dad and Mom a house. I am a very simple guy and don't require much.

Many people dream, and that is all they do: no plan of action, no motivation, or anything. I do realize if God's hand is not on it, then it will never work. I am truly a servant at heart and want to be used for God's glory.

Chapter 16 Mrs. Stancil, thank you!

I want to take the time to thank my future wife, friend, mother, children, intercessor, and so much more. I have waited for you for a long time. It was a Walt. I am grateful that you decided to go on this journey with me. You are a true gift from God, not just for me but for this world. I am thankful that God gifted you the way he did. God knew exactly what I needed in you as a mate. I know sometimes I might work your last never, but I guess we are stuck like crazy glue. We are bonded together until death do us part, and we will never speak of divorce ever. This is by God's design, and we will make it work. Be patient with me as I receive your genuine love. I thought I was loved before, but it was a lie.

I want you to be patient but firm with me as I let down my walls to let you in and become the man God ordained for your life. I can't wait for us to serve in the kingdom of God together, helping to change lives by the grace of God and by way of his Holy Spirit. I can see us now traveling the world with our kids and having the best life ever. I believe my latter shall be greater than my former, and you are a piece of that. I give you my devotion, commitment, and dedication to this union and pray God blesses it with a double portion of anointing so we can do his will and not our own.

I do thank God for you and plan on showing you how much each day, for the rest of our days, we are going to have the best life together, not comparable to anyone else. It will be uniquely designed. I can't wait to meet you, and when I do, I will know for sure that you are my assignment and I am yours. Until then, I am praying for you and our family. God's word does not come back void, but it accomplishes what he sent it to do. He can't lie ever, and he is a promise keeper.

Hold on, I am coming. With Love,
Derek Lamon

Chapter 17 Wait on God

Wait: to stay somewhere or stop doing something until someone comes or something happens.

I must say I was never a massive fan of this word at all. To be honest, most people are not either. I have learned over the years that the word wait requires the right attitude and state of mind. I was always a hyper person; I could not be still to save my life, constantly on the go from here to there and going nowhere. Waiting is a Godly discipline that most don't have, and it is a great gift to possess. I look back at some of the elders in my family, and they had this gift. They did not have the spiritual tools we have today, but they had this gift. I have since learned to just simply wait on God; moving out of his timing has cost me more than I was willing to pay. The old saying goes, good things come to those who wait.

It is true when you wait on God's perfect timing you are blessed beyond measure. Father God has a habit of doing the most awesome and mind-blowing things as we obey and trust him. Waiting requires a level of trust in the unknown and unseen as well. I blindly went into military service in 2001, and I can assure you I am still reaping the benefits of just simply waiting on God's perfect will. I did not know what I wanted to do in life, and I just prayed to God I would go anywhere and do anything He wanted me to do. God quickly put me to the test as I was sincere in my request, and off to the US Navy I went.

I am glad God did not give me things out of his timing because it would have destroyed me, I did marry at 38, and now some are like, wait, you wrote a letter thanking Mrs. Stancilyes, I did. I will speak about that marriage when God wants me to. I am now a divorced man at 45 and am still holding onto the promise that God gave me at the age of 19. The world we live in is a microwave generation. We want it all now, the car, house, career, all now often we are not mature enough to handle it all. These earthly and, most importantly, spiritual gifts have to be handled with the utmost care and respect, and if we don't know the value of a thing, we tend to abuse it and then lose.

I have definitely gotten a blessing and messed it up because I was not mature enough to manage it correctly. God is trying to teach us a lesson in all things so he can get the glory out of our lives at all times. I must say, if someone is sharing information with you, that can help you cherish that person no matter the delivery. If it is true, accept it. I am an advocate of eating the meat and spitting out the bones. I used to believe that lying would teach you and just let it; then, I matured and found out that if my father did something, it wouldn't work for him. Why would I go behind him and do the same? That is insane, but they may do it because they seek the wrong counsel.

Chapter 18 My setback was allowed for a comeback:

Well, yesterday, I received some bad news that I did not get the job I applied for because of my eyesight. I hate diabetes. It is a dreadful disease that can ravish the body with many afflictions. I wish I could have made better life choices concerning my health, but it is never too late to change. I need to become the best steward of what God has given me in all areas, especially this vessel. I wasted so much time being reckless, and it all has a cost attached to it. I must say, I was calm about the rejection and just prayed and knew that this opportunity was not for me. I had a plan, but God had another one and his plan is always the best, so I just learn the lesson

and keep it moving. God set apart a specific time for me these years, 2011 and 2012, to write so I could get this out to help someone else. I am certain many will identify with what I have gone through and how I made it out on the other side, healed, whole, and empowered. I have also learned not to share most things with folk because half don't care, and the others are waiting for you to fail.

I am excited about what God is going to do with this book that he ordained. I am grateful that he chose me to be the one to deliver to the nations. I want to be able to travel to different countries and share about God's goodness and his grace in all things. I can't take any credit for this because I did not even do well in English in high school. I did pass, but it was probably barely. 'God's word is true; he takes the foolish things of the world to confound the wise' 1 Cor 1:27. God, my creator and ruler, gets all the glory from this and anything else he empowers me to do through his Son Jesus Christ, my Lord, and savior.

I hope this encourages the reader to seek God for holiness and consecration and a life pleasing to God through our bodies. And that if you have sinned and fallen short, you can repent and not go that way again ever and be delivered from that ungodly sexual soul tie in Jesus's name. I love you all with the love of God. May he bless you and keep you, and may his face shine upon you.

Sincerely Yours,

Derek Lamon

Conclusion

I am thankful for allowing God to use me for his glory, I want to add I am not perfect, and I still make mistakes, but by his grace, I move on continually. I believe some of us are destined to carry heavier loads than others in this life. I am reminded of this verse: Ecclesiastes 9:11 'I returned, and saw under the sun, that the race is not to the swift, nor the battle to the strong, neither yet bread to the wise, nor yet riches to men of understanding, nor yet favor to men of skill; but time and chance happened to them all.' The assignment that God gives is about endurance we will all face many trials and tests.

I believe God is looking for a remnant of people who will do this as well. Luke 9:23, 'And he said to them all, if any man will come after me, let him deny himself, and take up his cross daily, and follow me.' God qualifies the call so those who feel like God could never use me that is a lie from Satan, the Father of all lies and all that is false.

I believed, received, and conceived the enemy's lies for many years, and it was to my detriment. I am telling you, yes, that if God is faithful to his word over my life, he will do the same for you if you hold onto him and the promise that he made; he is always faithful.

I love you all with the love of God through his Son, Jesus Christ, my Lord and SAVIOR!!!

Derek Lamon

Sex
is
Not
Love
Workbook

Expose:

To uncover or allow to be open in the air.

This definition is very on point. First, it uncovers well. You may ask, "Uncovers what?" Anything and everything that is hidden may be pornography, masturbation, group sex, gluttony. It doesn't matter what vice we've all had, and some of us still have one or more that we're working on or ignoring, this is very true.

God, by way of the Holy Spirit, gave me these stories:

David& Bathsheba 2 Samuel 11: Uncovering what is buried beneath.

I know some may be familiar with this story of betrayal, murder, adultery, and the ploy to cover it all up. You see, I can relate to covering things up to identify with David. I will give you some history of the King of Israel. He was handpicked by a Prophet of God and was not even included in the lineup of suitors for the position.

I am encouraged here because even when others forget, God will and always remember me. I can recall the verse that states,

"And God remembered Noah." (Genesis 8:1). David was a lowly sheep keeper, being their protector, provider, and overall caregiver. He did his job well and was passionate about it. Wherever your passion is, most times, your anointing is there as well.

David had not gone to battle with the rest of his company. He was walking one evening along the roof, and he noticed a beautiful woman. David became interested in who she was, so he sent word to find out who she was, and he found out she was another man's wife.

David did not care. This was his 3rd mistake, and he lay down with her. She became pregnant, and David started a plan to cover his actions, and this is what the most powerful man did at the time of the sinful act. David realized that his attempts to get Uriah to sleep with his wife, all failed. Uriah was a man of integrity and would not forsake his company to go and have a night of pleasure.

Uriah even told David he would not do it to his face. He stood for what he believed, and unfortunately, it cost him his life. I want to stand by the Godly principles he has bestowed upon me like this man.

David wrote a letter to the Commander of the Camp that Uriah was attached to and told him to put him out front and pull back the rest of the company so Uriah would die, and he did. Uriah died that day, and David assumed that all he did was over and done with until he got a visit from the Prophet Nathan. The Prophet began to tell David a story.

David became enraged when Nathan was done and said the man who did this would surely die. Nathan said to him, "You are that man," and immediately David repented. Nathan told him that God despised what he did and gave instructions on what would happen to him as a result.

When we sin knowingly or unknowingly, consequences are the end result. It does not matter if we know or not. Most times, we choose not to recognize our wrong behavior.

Deception has ravaged the church. We think we are ok, but the scriptures say that we, as believers, righteousness is as of filthy rags and that we would barely make it in. We can

never get free from what we will not admit, accept and ask for forgiveness, and lastly, CHANGE!!!!

God does not look at our outward appearance. He looks at our hearts and determines what our true intentions are, and

believe me, your actions are a direct pathway to your heart. We can fool everyone else but he knows all and sees all. I could fool everyone but not people who have God's spirit.

David did eventually get connected back to God, but God left him for a season. David still pursued him through, and God blessed him with another son. Solomon and David went on to reign successfully. This is a picture-perfect story of how God can redeem even in the most horrible and low and dark places. I am glad that Jesus went to Calvary for me so that I can be free from my past sins and present and future. He is awesome, and I am so joyful about that.

Educate:

Give intellectual, moral, and social instruction to (someone, especially children), typically at a school or university.

Like many who went to school for twelve years to get a diploma, to be honest, I could have cared less about school. I wanted to drop out because I did not like it at all. I was bullied, and I was also mean because of it. I had the worst attitude, and you all will see why later on in the book. I did graduate on time at the bottom of my class and was not even excited about it. I didn't understand the importance of that diploma my mother, who did not graduate but received her GED later.

Acts 9: The Story of Saul's Conversion to Paul: Transformation

And as he journeyed, he came near Damascus: and suddenly their shined round about him a light from heaven: Encounter with Jesus

And he fell to the earth, and heard a voice saying unto him, Saul, Saul, why persecutes thou me? Jesus tells him exactly what sin he is carrying out.

And he said, Who art thou, Lord? And the Lord said, I am Jesus whom thou persecute: it is hard for thee to kick against the pricks. Jesus makes it very clear who he is speaking to.

And he trembling and astonished said, Lord, what wilt thou have me to do? And the Lord said unto him, Arise, and go into the city, and it shall be told thee what thou must do.

Saul received his first task, and it was a simple one, just going kind of like Abraham went.

Saul did as he was instructed, and a disciple named Ananias had a vision from the Lord about Saul. He was told to go and lay his hands on Saul's eyes so that he could receive sight, but Ananias was reluctant. Jesus reassured him that Saul was about to be used for the glory of God. Ananias followed instructions and went to where Saul was, where he had been waiting for him. Ananias called him brother as he lay hands on his eyes for him to get his sight back. Now, he would see clearly. The Bible states it was as if scales fell from his eyes.

I was led to Saul, later called Paul, because he was a scholar by his own admission. He knew Jewish law like the back of his hand. He was a very intelligent man and a determined one as well. I believe God chose him because he knew Paul would serve him wholeheartedly and was sold out to the cause of Christ as Messiah. Paul had to forget or at least put aside all he knew in the natural world and go to the school of the Holy Spirit to be led by Him and not his intellect at all.

I have learned, just like Paul, that we have to go to the same school of the Holy Spirit. If we are ever going to be used by God, we must abandon all of our carnal thinking. We must forget how we used to live; this only causes a war within, and the Holy Spirit is a gentleman. He will never force His will upon us at all. He will move onto the willing vessel. Paul quickly gave way to God to cause his drastic conversion; he did not think about it at all; he just surrendered his will to God. I think it is very wise to do the same, and we will have the same victory that Paul had throughout his Christian walk.

Empowered:

God the Father gave Jesus' power for this assignment by way of the Holy Spirit.

Matthew 3: 16,17,4:1-11 KJV

I think most of us don't really get that Jesus was fully human and fully God. It is hard for us to wrap our heads around the fact that God did dwell among us. Matthew 3:16-17 states that Jesus was baptized, and when he came out of the water, he received the Spirit of God on him, and it set like a dove. He was empowered for the temptation he was about to endure in Matthew 4:1-11. Jesus passed every test because he knew the truth, and he did not attempt to fight Satan at all; he only used the word of God.

Satan started kind of subtle in trying to put doubt in him about who he was in God. Execute EXALTED Jesus on the cross Matthew 27:32-56

Jesus was led to the cross and was crucified; he did not murmur or complain about the pain, embarrassment, ridicule, and mocking at all. He endured and held his peace despite it all. How many of us can't even contain ourselves with a headache? We make every excuse of why we are negative in our situations and say I am only human, but guess what? So was Jesus. He was fully God and fully man. Hebrews 4:15 states that awe has a high priest who has felt what we feel now, and yet he did not sin. Jesus was equipped to execute the assignment on his life just like we have been. We must rely on the Holy Spirit daily to lead us and guide us into all truth as Jesus said he would. The suffering that tests and trials bring often produces the fruit that we need: diamonds are produced by pressure only. I now understand how Betty Wright prophetically said, "NO PAIN, NO GAIN." She says in the song to get something, you gotta give something. I may have given a hint of my age. God chooses regular men and women and uses them to do great exploits ex, David was a shepherd out with sheep, and Joseph was a spoiled kid who had to go through a process of eliminating himself to execute the dreams God gave him.

We must go through the same process to be able to execute the will and plan for our lives. I am now getting wisdom, knowledge, and understanding of my assignment and my book is one of them. God can and will use another. If we fail to comply with his plan/will for our lives, the anointing assignment will be passed to another. God's work will get done with or without us.

We must choose daily to execute God's plan for our lives, and we achieve that by doing exactly Matthew 6:33 33 But seek ye first the kingdom of God, and his righteousness and all these things shall be added unto you. I assure you that this method works because we are not depending on our own strengths, talents, intellect, money, or connections. Jesus accepted and completed the call on his life and now has the name above every name. I challenge you as the reader to find out exactly what plan God has for you because you will still be held accountable for whatever it is God called you to do. I pray that as you go through this workbook, it will challenge you to seek God with your whole heart.

Exalted:

1. (of a person or their rank or status) placed at a high or powerful level; held in high regard:

Philippians 2:9-11

Jesus left his heavenly position with authority and honor to come here to earth to fix what the first Adam messed up. Jesus did not think it beneath him to come down to the level of a mere flesh and blood baby. Jesus grew up as a human with an earthly father and mother as well and had to obey them like we were trained to do. Jesus passed every test that came his way as an adult. After he went into the wilderness, he came out ready to work.

66 Philippians 2:9 says Wherefore God also hath highly exalted him, and given him a name which is above every name:"

The next verses also state that every knee will bow, and the tongue will confess that Jesus Christ is Lord of all. This includes all the people who never believed and mocked Jesus as a fraud. They will see one day that he is who he says he is and that God is not a liar at all! What a wonderful day and painful day for those who rejected the truth of the Messiah.

God has exalted us as well; he tells us we are seated in heavenly places Ephesians 2:6 We as believers are in Christ as we obey God the Father through his commands and decrees. Jesus is the blueprint we need to follow to get total victory over every enemy that comes across our path.

We are given many suggestions to follow God through Jesus Christ. He is the way of the truth and the light. I know it has worked for my good many times. I did not know where life was taking me, but I put my trust in God through his Son, and I was led down an ordained path. I implore you to do as Jesus did and lay down your life and follow God. It will be the best decision ever, and no, it will not always feel good, but that is okay. We are led by faith anyway.

Execute:

Carry out or put into effect (a plan, order, or course of action.

Luke 22:47-65 King James Version

47   And while he yet spake, behold a multitude, and he that was called Judas, one of the twelve, went before them, and drew near unto Jesus to kiss him.

48   But Jesus said unto him, Judas, betrayest thou the Son of man with a kiss?

49   When they which were about him saw what would follow, they said unto him, Lord, shall we smite with the sword?

50   And one of them smote the servant of the high priest and cut off his right ear.

51   And Jesus answered and said, Suffer ye thus far. And he touched his ear and healed him.

Then Jesus said unto the chief priests, and captains of the temple, and the elders, which were come to him, be ye come out, as against a thief, with swords and staves?

When I was daily with you in the temple, ye stretched forth no hands against me: but this is your hour, and the power of darkness.

52   Then took they him, and led him, and brought him into the high priest's house. And Peter followed afar off.

53   And when they had kindled a fire amid the hall, and were set down together, Peter sat down among them.

54   But a certain maid beheld him as he sat by the fire, and earnestly looked upon him, and said, this man was also with him.

55   And he denied him, saying, Woman, I know him not.

56   And after a little while another saw him, and said, Thou art also of them. And Peter said, Man, I am not.

57   And about the space of one hour after another

58   confidently affirmed, saying, of truth this fellow also was with him: for he is a Galilaean.

59   And Peter said, Man, I know not what thou sayest. And immediately, while he yet Spake, the cock crew.

60   And the Lord turned and looked upon Peter. And Peter remembered the word of the Lord, how he had said unto him, Before the cock crow, thou shalt deny me thrice.

61   And Peter went out and wept bitterly.

62   And the men that held Jesus mocked him and smote him.

63   And when they had blindfolded him, they struck him on the face, and asked him, saying, Prophesy, who is it that smote thee?

64   And many other things blasphemously Spake they against him.

Jesus did not run from his assignment, and he knew what it entailed; he stuck it out and finished well for my sake and every person born and unborn. Jesus was physically, mentally, verbally, and psychologically attacked, but he did not waver in his faith that God had a plan for this situation. He did get weary in the garden of Gethsemane, but he kept it moving and was determined to get to the cross. He did, and one of his last statements was found in John 19:30. He states that it is finished.

Father God, in Jesus's name, I ask that the person reading this now surrender his/her will and accept and agree with your will. I ask that if the reader does not know you as a personal savior, they will ask you to come into their heart right now and be saved from their sins. In Jesus's name, I pray, Amen.

Questions:

1. Do you need to forgive anyone, including yourself?

2. Do you self-blame, and why?

3. Have you ever loved properly according to God?

4. What small change could you make to ensure a victorious path?

5. How is your heart?

6. Can you be accountable to anyone and be vulnerable?

7. What area are you not letting God in?

8. Do you have trust issues?

9. Do you have Mommy and Daddy wounds?

10. Do you ever see yourself healed, whole, and thriving?